To Chigozie

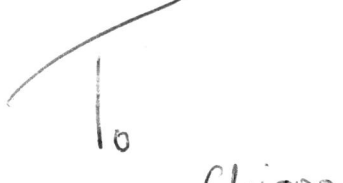

O.C. VINCE

================================

Unleash

Your Life's

Greatness

================================

The Real Guide

To Transforming

Business Ideas into Reality

Unleash

Your Life's

Greatness

O.C. Vince

www.ocvince.net
First published in Great Britain with TamaRe House, April 2011

Copyright © O.C. Vince, 2011

This book is copyright under the Berne Convention.
No part of this book is to be reproduced, reprinted, copied, or stored in retrieval systems of any type, except by written permission from the Author. Parts of this book may however be used only in reference to support related documents.
All rights reserved.

The right of O. C. Vince to be identified as author of this work has been asserted in accordance with sections 77 and 78 of the Copyright, Designs and Patents Act, 1988.

A CIP catalogue record for this book is available from the British Library.
This employs acid free paper and meets all ANSI standards for archival quality paper.

ISBN 9781906169-31-2

TamaRe House
25 Brixton Station Road, London, SW9 8PB, United Kingdom
044 (0)844 357 2592, info@tamarehouse.com, www.tamarehouse.com

Printed and bound in Great Britain

Dedication

Dedicated to my parents, Mr. Francis Onyekwelu and Mrs. Cecilia Onyekwelu, and to colleagues, teachers, friends and comrades, both living and dead for all the inspirational life and business intelligence they formally and informally taught me from an early age and to Nkiru, Fide, Ogor and Bona's coaching. It is them who revealed to me, most of all I have learned from teenage age to practice unleashing life's greatness.

Thank you for purchasing this book. Apply it to your life, and transform your business ideas into reality.

Thanks to Mdhamiri á Nkemi of Jacket Design for my cover page graphics

CONTENT

Author's Note 1
Foreword 2
Introduction 6

Ch 01. Action Speaks Louder 12
Ch 02. Let's Talk Business Ideas 17
Ch 03. Nurturing Your Business Enterprise Idea................. 27
Ch 04. Winning Attitude 41
Ch 05. Personal Development 50
Ch 06. Choosing Business Location 58
Ch 07. Sourcing Start-Up funds 66
Ch 08. Marketing Your Business 89
Ch 09. Your Business Starts Trading 108
Ch 10. A Final Note 119

Glossary of Terms 123
Praise for Unleash your Life's Greatness........................ 129
About the Author 131

Author's Note

Unleash Your Life's Greatness contains messages, illustrated with case studies, to support you in improving your 'Life Value' as you transform your ideas into a successful start to your business enterprise.

This book will provide for you a step-by-step guide to achieving success. It will assist you in gaining a mindset that demonstrates that:

'Yesterday's business challenge is a memory, tomorrow's business opportunity is a mystery and today's business idea is the right one, at the right time, to start tapping into the gifts within you that are waiting to be unleashed.'

O.C. Vince is the pseudonym of Vince Onyekwelu, who used his academic and practical experience in business management, corporate training and enterprise development to write this business self help and inspirational book. **Unleash Your Life's Greatness** will support, motivate and inspire new and existing business entrepreneurs to transform their ideas into successful business ventures.

Foreword

Jane Francis wasn't always a great public speaker. In fact she was one of the worst in her school when she was growing up. Over time, though, through practice she became rather good at it and became the captain of her national team.

It was the grand finale of a long awaited public speaking competition and Jane felt prepared mentally and physically. She wanted to ensure that her team would triumph, so as to bring glory to her country and to make herself proud.

Although she had learnt how to speak with passion, she was also afraid that she would let down the entire team. She was afraid of trying and scared of failing, all at the same time.

These thoughts affected her confidence and performance in the first round of speech and, all too soon, it was her turn for the second round.

It seemed to her, while she stood at the podium, that her team, her fans and the country were waiting at the edges of their seats. Jane knew it was her last chance to win the public speaking competition.

In those last, split seconds, with her heart pounding, she made up her mind to use an emotional, compassionate and persuasive speaking style to impress the judges. It was a style which she had practised so hard to master, but was scared of attempting.

Foreword

It was a style of public speaking that was aimed at making her sound convincing and believable.

Believable! That was the operative word. Yes, she thought, she too needed to believe in herself!

She stepped out onto the speaking platform and looked at the panel of judges. After taking a deep breath, she cleared her throat and started speaking. She spoke with a clear tone, filled with compassion and emotion. Her humble family background influenced the topic and the emotions which filled her speech. She spoke of how her parents worked almost eighteen hours a day, seven days of the week to give her the best start in life and to enable her to become the best that she could be. Her speech caused tears to come to the eyes of not a few members of the audience. Her convincing body language and the variety of pitches she used whilst speaking of the tough stages of her childhood was overwhelming for all present. The judges watched and listened in complete silence and absorbed interest, noting how she managed her speaking time and maintained eye contact with all of them.

When she had finished, she was awarded the maximum score available, no one had ever yet achieved this in the competition.

Her team won the trophy.

Her new speaking style became the talk of the competition

because she had been able to transform her speaking idea into a real performance, which brought herself, her team and her country success.

She had overcome her fears and limitations but had **unleashed her life's greatness.**

I urge you to take your life skills and your ideas seriously; using them to succeed in the business of your choice, in your chosen career or in your Life. This is not a trial run for your life.

Today is the time to make the right decision, seek for support and leverage your 'Life Value' to **Unleash Your Life's Greatness.**

Sandra Mottoh,
Director Bank of America
Merrill Lynch
March 2011

Introduction

Believe in your Brain Child

Introduction

Believe in your Brain Child

YOU HAVE TO BELIEVE IN YOUR BRAIN CHILD. This is your ability to activate what your character is comfortable with, to assist you to find and use your own unique idea or brainchild to go on to **unleash your life's greatness**. This will motivate you to:

Live life and not allow life to live you

Your brainchild is a product of your creative work or thought. The beauty that lives inside you is willing and waiting. It is a worthy way to express yourself gainfully.

Stop postponing your life's greatness. It is time for you to start taking the right decisions for you to activate the business enterprise ideas within.

The urgency of NOW demands you tap into and unlock your God-given-talents. These talents, as gifts to your life, need to be unwrapped creatively, positively and actively. Transform these great ideas and start-up your business enterprise. Your ideas are not there, within you, by accident!

Unleash Your Life's Greatness will give you the inspirational steps needed to enrich your business start-up and solutions that will answer the majority of your business set-up questions.

Unleash Your Life's Greatness contains positive tools that will furnish you with procedures to help you move forward from where you are today, towards where you need to be.

Unleash Your Life's Greatness will assist you to take your ideas into your business enterprise successfully, sustainably and steadily, as well as affordably. There are no single books that respond to all possible business enterprise questions, however, **Unleash Your Life's Greatness** has the edge over many and will, hopefully, enable you to fulfil most of your expectations about your business needs through being able to provide most of the answers to your business set up enquiries.

Whilst most of your questions on transforming business ideas to reality are responded to, naturally, given the rapidly changing business environment, new questions emerge every day.

I believe this book will bring to you the energy, enthusiasm and experience which provokes thought, opens the mind and affirms your life. You will find the language of **Unleash Your Life's Greatness** easy to follow, easy to understand and easy to relate to your everyday business ideas. It is written with knowledge and insight of the business arena and from daily experience in business environments. All of this and more, with everyday business language!

This book is designed, planned and written with you, the reader, in mind. **Unleash Your Life's Greatness** is written for

pre-starts: those who are thinking, hoping and dreaming of starting a business enterprise. It is also written for ***post-starts***, where it is directed at increasing the awareness of opportunities and pitfalls for those who have already taken the first steps in creating their own business enterprise.

Unleash your Life's Greatness will positively position you wherever you seek to be: as a sole trader, limited company, partnership or a limited liability partnership. Most importantly it will position you as a business woman or business man.

Look at the example of a spider that positions its web in the most perfect place, in order to efficiently target and trap its prey. You will also need to locate yourself advantageously and communicate with your all your clients, consider your competition and master your market.

In business, be ready to ***be the change*** that your customers and competitors follow rather than allowing ***them*** to be the change that you follow.

This book is a collection of over fifteen years of commercial and personal experience and achievements in business enterprise; personal development; business training and advisory services; as well as personal success in business enterprise internationally.

I am a seasoned, enterprise consultant who has successfully mentored, trained and have been a consultant for small, medium and large private and public organisations across three

Introduction

continents: Africa, Asia and Europe.

Importantly, I have started my own businesses and so understand the challenges, values and the victories faced by the average entrepreneur.

Whilst I was delivering business start-up seminars in South Africa, I felt compelled to pull together my several years' of experience into a comprehensive book to reach out to all those that seek to understand business basics in a friendly, accessible design.

After two years of attempting to reschedule my life to find the space to start writing this book; I finally put pen to paper on Christmas Eve of 2009.

I put my idea of writing this book into action and as a result, after a few sleepless nights over the layout, these ideas turned into a real enterprise.

I believe this book will further energise your business enterprise ideas and inspire you. This will be generated from an abundance of practical, positive and priceless steps drawn from the width, depth and breadth of a summary of the ways and means possible to realise your business enterprise vision.

You make think your ideas are too simple. Simple ideas, however, are what great entrepreneurs have, in the past, activated and transformed into great business empires. Simple, in this context, is good.

Some of these great entrepreneurs and business owners transformed the same kind of business enterprise ideas that you may have. Today, people who have had business ideas but not acted upon them may instead be applying for jobs, being assessed at interviews and striving to become employees for business enterprise owners who have acted on *their* business ideas.

At some stage in your life you may have been an employee but there is nothing wrong in striving to be your own boss.

Something is not right, in your world, when you overlook your life's greatness. There are talents within you, waiting to be explored and brought forth, a possible brainchild waiting to be born which will help you to realise your purpose. It will enable you to be the best you can be, for yourself, for your generation and for your destiny.

Chapter 1

Action Speaks Louder...

Chapter 1

Action Speaks Louder

Your Ideas Needs Action

ENTREPRENEURS, WHO ACT ON THEIR BRAINCHILD NOW, will, in the future, be less disappointed by the things that they did than those who do nothing. Take action on your ideas to discover and fulfil your purpose in life.

It has once been said that there is a reason why the heart beats and there is a reason why the river flows. This simply means that the heart and the river fulfil their purpose in the scheme of things. What is your purpose? When will you **unleash it to find your life's greatness**?

How long will it take you to realise what impact the uncertainties of the current global economy is having on you? The fact that the gap between the rich and the poor is growing and that the few jobs that are available are being applied for by applicants in their thousands is no longer news.

Be encouraged to think widely, creatively and outside the box and **unleash your life's greatness** through the setting up of your own business enterprise. Your entrepreneurial idea could be what thousands, if not millions, are waiting for YOU to develop, in order for them to flourish. So unleashing your business potential is also a duty and responsibility!

Great, creative entrepreneurs and business owners such as Oprah Winfrey, Simon Cowell, and Richard Branson; as well as those who found success as a result of participating in TV reality shows such as the **Apprentice** and **Dragons Den** are everyday people who simply invested in their own, creative potential.

They found success by making active use of their enterprise ideas by putting these ideas forward, with faith in themselves. They promoted their ideas, practiced them and participated in the TV shows and the rest is history!

The lessons we can learn from these people is that they had ideas to:

- Explore and understand their life purpose and action their belief
- Acknowledge and transform weakness into greatness
- Create solutions for everyday problems
- Create products and services that can attract more clients
- Re-create an existing product or service to attract new users

They achieved this by:

- Tapping into their power of creating solutions to problems
- Using their skills, expertise and aptitudes
- Transforming their fears into faith and belief
- Putting into action their purpose to set them on course to achieving their dreams. Believing in possibilities rather than impossibilities

It is fine to call your brainchild by any of the names that make sense to you, such as: business idea or thought, flash bulb or vision. The most important thing is that the term has a real meaning to you.

There is a saying that we all dream but we don't all dream equally. We do not act equally either. Some people dream at night and resolve, in the back of their minds, to wake up and then do not take action to transform their dreams into realities.

No action taken means no success achieved

However, some people dream by day with their minds alert and eyes wide open and they take creative, constructive and complete actions to transform their dreams into realities. These realities may result in a positive impact on society. They attract customers to buy into the service or product/s and bring success to their life. They certainly keep a smile on their face ... all the way to the bank!

A good business idea alone, however, is worth nothing more than a tool in your hand. It is worth nothing until you take creative, calculated and constructive steps towards transforming it from an initial idea into an actual product or service that customers love to buy and/or use repeatedly. The service or product needs to be beneficial, meet the needs of target customers and fully cover the cost of production, so as to make profit.

A business idea is an opportunity when it becomes a product or a service.

A product or service which is:

- Durable
- Attractive
- Timely
- Adds value

Stay positive and protect your business idea because it can be said that the best business enterprise ideas or opportunities have not yet been explored and so are not yet in use. Your business idea could be one of these. Think about how to translate your business ideas into what customers and the marketplace both want and need in order to enable you to **unleash your life's greatness.**

Chapter 2

Let's Talk Business Ideas

Chapter 2

Let's Talk Business Ideas

Your Ideas Has Purpose

WHEN BUSINESS ENTERPRISE IDEAS come into your mind, their purpose might be to provide solutions that you can apply to solve particular problems that you and those close to you are experiencing or have experienced in your community and society.

A business idea might be one which you believe is capable of adding value or improving the processes used to carry out tasks such as how to manage your family, to care for your children and to strike a good work/life balance. The ideas you have may seem local but can be nurtured into becoming global ideas. This supports you in thinking of the global impact of your business idea whilst acting local. This is true even if you are permanently resident in a particular town or post code at present.

There are times when you have had ideas that could potentially have elevated you from where you are today to where you need to be in life. The truth of the matter is this: when a business idea comes into your mind, it arrives there for a specific time and for a specific purpose. If you fail to act on this idea, after a given time, someone else will take that action.

With most business ideas, after a certain time, there is the possibility that someone, somewhere may come up with that same idea. This means, the sooner you use your idea, the better for you. Why wait until someone else does?

Let us use the following scenario. It is one which I usually draw upon whilst delivering business training seminars. It is the story of a domestic cat, who, when it looks at itself in a mirror, instead of seeing a mere cat; it sees a reflection of a tiger. There is also the story of a lion, which looks at itself in a mirror and instead of seeing the mighty king of the jungle; it only sees the reflection of a simple, domestic cat.

Have you asked yourself, "Who am I? What is my life's purpose and what business enterprise will best meet my personal character?" Are you a domestic cat that thinks, acts, values and sees something huge and successful in yourself like a lion?

On the other hand, are you a larger than life personality but you think, act and value yourself as too insignificant to become successful?

Do you see those business enterprise ideas in your mind as the mighty lion or do you see them as the small cat? This doesn't mean the domestic cat is not a formidable creature in its own right, but, rather, that when the strength of a single domestic

Chapter 2   Let's Talk Business Ideas

cat is compared to that of a lion; it is clear which has greater strength, style and status in the animal kingdom.

There are distinguishing factors and characteristics, which separate a 'cat' from a 'lion' in the world of business. There are those people that creatively, consistently and constructively act on their business ideas and those that do not. The difference is that the contenders make history by exploring their ideas and subsequently acting on them. Alternatively, there are the pretenders, who, through little or no action, often experience failure and give excuses as to why they never took consistent and constructive actions.

How do you see yourself is another distinguishing factor. The type of information you feed your mind and the kind of people you spend your time with, influences the way you see yourself. Do you hang out with dream-makers, believers and winners or are your friends and associates dream-killers, quitters and procrastinators? Also, be aware of the picture you paint in your own mind of your abilities and willingness to use either improvisation or original thought to find your purpose in business or in any profession. This is because there is a difference between pure creativity and innovation; in that with creativity, you build an idea from scratch, while innovation can be seen as improving something already in existence.

Learn to act on the skills and strengths that live within you and conquer your weaknesses quicker, faster and better before someone else identifies them for you. We all have weaknesses, we need to be aware of them and work to reduce them.

Let us apply another scenario I often use. Think of looking at things from the result or the outcome first and then work backwards, step by step, to the start. Let us use the act of brushing the teeth in the morning. Think, now, of what kind of consequences may result, in terms of dental treatment caused by how you habitually care for your teeth. How would you avoid a painful, dental filling by a dentist? You would need to go back to your everyday habit of dental care and ensure that, over time, you take action as soon as the very first sign of plaque on your teeth appeared. In this way you would not end up paying an expensive dental bill and experiencing the associated pain.

How do friends and family describe you in terms of transforming ideas into reality? Do they describe you as a dream-killer, procrastinator or a winner? Are you described as a dream-fulfiller that makes good things happen?

The above could assist you to understand the different reasons to motivate you to either take action or not take action. Some of these reasons may be described as: 'PUSH or PULL' factors.

The Pull Factors – These are '*Direct Drivers*' or reasons that draw you towards actions to achieve an intention (Opportunity Entrepreneurs):

- Independence

Chapter 2   Let's Talk Business Ideas

- Achievement
- Recognition
- Personal development
- Personal wealth

The Push Factors – These are '*Indirect Drivers*' or reasons that move you away from a situation, to achieve something, (Necessity Entrepreneurs):

- Unemployment
- Job insecurity
- Disagreement with current management
- Inability to 'fit into' an organization

Let us look at another scenario: six years ago a colleague of mine had a business idea that came into her mind. The idea was to diversify the way people view photographs by having an automatically rotating photo frame showing slide pictures of family, friends, pets and places of interest.

'When a business idea comes into your mind, it came in for a purpose and if you fail to do something with it, someone else will take it and act on it because most business ideas, as a rule, after a certain time, will move from one person to another, near or far.'

> *'Your mind is better than the best computer and will always be the best source of original ideas, innovations and memories. Think of the fantastic ideas that lie buried in the graveyard, unachieved.'*

Historically, these photos are stood, upright in plastic, metal or wooden frames, placed upon shelves and tables or hung on walls and show only one photo image at a time.

This colleague of mine had an idea about how to transform a photo frame into a modern single frame, which would exhibit more than one photo at timed intervals.

We can appreciate that in preference to having to look at a single image continuously, an enhancement would be an innovation that allows one to view several different images over a set time period.

She failed, however, to act on her fantastic idea and, after some time, it was simply forgotten about. Surprisingly, or perhaps not so, given the earlier rule given, exactly the same product has been designed, manufactured and patented by *someone else* and is a million dollar business today.

It would be so easy to blame her for failing to take her idea seriously but it is possible your business ideas have a similar

Chapter 2   Let's Talk Business Ideas

story.

The truth is, you do have potential business ideas in your mind and, if not used, these ideas will definitely leave your mind and try another mind that is better organised, better focused and active enough to transform these ideas into reality.

In a world, of fantastic, multifunctional technology gadgets like iPod™, Blackberry™ and iPhone™ as well as the various android phones or digital voice recorders that are available, there is a range to choose from to save voiced ideas as digital and then printable records, almost at the same time that you have them! You can also take down written notes. These can then be set as goals that you need to achieve. Paper notebooks, jotters and diaries are not yet out dated, however, they are still very useful. Use them to make notes or write down your ideas as they come into your mind to avoid forgetting and therefore losing them.

Once these ideas are written down, organise your time each week or each month, or at a regular interval which suits you, to spend at least an hour or two to do a SWOT analysis (see below), of these ideas to understand if you have the will, the ability and the resources to directly work on them. If you feel that you continue, then go for it, and start the process. If you feel that you really cannot progress; if you have explored the possibilities of developing the will, ability and resources and still find yourself at a total loss, then, and only then, see if you can sell your idea on. You can do this as it is, not yet developed, or if you can develop the idea to a more attractive level, then do so and sell it for good money.

There are business entrepreneurs at trade fairs, conferences or, perhaps, in an office near you, who have the capital and who are seeking innovative or original business ideas to invest in. Remember that an entrepreneur is a person who organises business operations, especially those involving some element of risk taking. One or more of them could be willing to negotiate with you to buy the idea and/or offer you a contract to play a role in the further development of the idea into a real business.

SWOT stands for:

S: Strengths:
- (A list of one's strong points in terms of abilities, skills and assets which are used to develop growth) –
- What have you done to identify your personal skills, assets and abilities and how are you developing and using these to full advantage?

W: Weaknesses:
- (A list of weak points: in terms of inabilities, skill gaps, lack of assets, which have to be addressed to enable growth) –

Chapter 2   Let's Talk Business Ideas

- How have you identified your weaknesses and what are you doing to change them to positively benefit your life, career and livelihood?

O: Opportunities:

- (A list of possible opportunities, openings or 'niches' which the competition may not appear to have exploited) -
- When are you going to start using your vision to take advantage of possibilities presented to you and to move you from where you are now to where you need to be to start, sustain and succeed in your business?

T: Threats:

- (A list of factors which could restrict growth, hinder improvement and ultimately lead to a loss of status) -
- What challenges do you face and how do they impact upon your ability to transform business ideas into reality?

By forming the habit of writing your business ideas down and then doing a SWOT analysis, you will understand your business ideas better. You can identify what you can do to make that process, product or service more efficient, effective and economically useful to your target customers. This will help your business become financially profitable and worthwhile.

Chapter 3

Nurturing Your Business Enterprise Ideas

Chapter 3

Nurturing Your Business Enterprise Idea

Excellent Business Support

DEVELOPING YOUR BUSINESS ENTERPRISE IDEA is an important task to add creativity, style and substance to your initial business enterprise idea. *Nurturing* your business idea is a timeless process that continues even after you have started the business. Business ideas come and go with time but nurturing your business idea is a continuous business attitude.

The Oxford Advanced Learner's Dictionary defines attitude as, 'the way you think, feel about and behave towards a subject'. Attitude, it is said, determines your business aptitude. The same Dictionary defines aptitude as, 'natural ability or skill at doing something'. Aptitude, in turn, determines your business altitude, it is said. Here, business altitude refers to how high or advanced in progress your business reaches. Business altitude refers to how high one can reach with one's business growth, development or profitability.

How do you think and behave in the face of everyday business challenges? Do you have the faith and the fight to succeed, or do you freeze, fear and take flight or hide away? It is important to learn in business enterprise to face challenges and find solutions, rather than take flight and think the problem will just disappear.

What is your natural ability or skill profile and how does your character fit with your selected business idea? Understanding how your personal character matches your business idea is a practical tool for understanding how you can be passionate and motivated enough to wake up each morning, whilst looking forward to an exciting business day.

'Your passion alone is very important but will never, single-handedly, nurture your business idea into a successful and sustainable enterprise.'

How high do you see yourself fly? How determined are you to see beyond your ideas and fears and take dominion and fly so high because the sky is no longer the limit: the sky has become the starting point?

Being at this point is the baseline from which you break through limitations, achieve your goals and support and sustain your business's **Unique Selling Point**, popularly called the USP.

It is most important and natural for you to be passionate about your business idea. Do remember that passion alone is very

Chapter 3 Nurturing Your Business Enterprise Idea

important but will never, single-handedly, nurture your business idea into a successful and sustainable enterprise.

The steps that you will need to take to support and sustain your business idea survival depend on how you can manage factors such as passion, knowledge, money, time, government legislation and people, as well as manage any barriers to success.

Attending business start-up seminars and workshops are good ways of nurturing your business ideas. Business seminars and workshops do, however, vary in areas of focus, so be diligent in your choice of them, making sure they are applicable to you and where you are in terms of stage of business development. So it makes a lot of sense to first attend the appropriate business workshops by speaking to qualified business advisors who will further enhance your passion, knowledge, skills and help you to understand your target market before you even think of registering your business name. Once you register your business name with the appropriate government agency, it comes with immediate tax responsibilities. This is a serious commitment which requires you to be sufficiently motivated to see you through the necessary paperwork involved in your chosen business sector.

Throughout my years of experience, I have seen business men and women struggle once they register their business name, without understanding the responsibilities involved. It is like putting the cart before the horse. The horse is meant to pull the cart for the journey to start, as it has not been known for carts to pull horses.

A while ago, another colleague of mine had an idea to set up a leather business. The leather was to be imported into the United Kingdom from Brazil.

She was so passionate about her business idea that she spent endless time attending business seminars and workshops that dealt only with taxation and accounting.

This is not to say that these seminars are not relevant to business start-up.

However, at the early stages, with little or no experience in business, it would have added more value if she applied the simple rule of **'First things first'**.

This would have been achieved by doing what was more important, or

> **'Nurturing your entrepreneurial ideas is a continuous business <u>attitude</u> that develops your business <u>aptitude</u>, which then determines your business <u>altitude</u>.'**

critical to establishing the business. This would have included: asking for basic information on where best to locate the business; finding out how to fund the business; exploring the market to find out what the demand is for leather and

Chapter 3   Nurturing Your Business Enterprise Idea

researching the range of finished products for which the leather will be put to use and so on.

This colleague of mine would have benefited from speaking to a business adviser; attending business awareness seminars or workshops that were focused on her area of business and conducting research using libraries; established businesses in the field and selective relevant resource centres. She would, by doing this, gain an understanding in specific and general business knowledge issues in her selected business area to respond to questions such as:

- Why the choice of a leather business?
- Which region, age group and gender are her target customers?
- What type of business legal status is the best to register?
- What choice of business name, logo, slogan and elevator pitch to choose?
- What is the competition in that market segment?
- Which area of the city would be best to set up in and why?
- Are there current European Union (EU) legislations with adverse effects or impacts on importing from a non-EU country like Brazil?

- Are her Portuguese language skills sufficient for effective communication in the Brazilian business environment?

'A failure to plan your business is planning to fail in your business.'

The above list, though not limited to these questions, can provoke thoughts and actions in the most helpful direction to the business owner.

There are also business advisors that you can book appointments with on a one-to-one basis. A good business adviser will use various methods e.g. coaching and mentoring to work with you and support you to choose the necessary initial seminars and workshops to attend. They will also support in developing some of the following key components of your business.

A Business Plan:

This is an important document that precisely and clearly describes, in a logical order, your business idea. It is this which people outside of, as well as inside, your business, will use to judge its likely business success. A failure to plan your business is planning to fail in your business.

Your business plan should aim to:

Chapter 3   Nurturing Your Business Enterprise Idea

- Prove to funding organisations that your business idea is viable and will generate sustainable return
- Capture the long term objectives and set out a road map to success
- Give a clear direction for the future
- Communicate your vision to key stakeholders
- Help you save time, stress and financial difficulties later

A business plan describes your business objectives, justification, strategies, market analysis and financial planning. The business plan contains every detail about your enterprise: from where the business will be based to where you will find your first customer. It also functions as a design for future development of your business that potential investors will want to read before they consider lending money to you. Although it is in this way descriptive, it does not mean that you give away confidential, business practices that your competition might use so as to develop a competitive edge against you!

A Business plan is, nonetheless, flexible. You can innovate within it and change tactics within it as long as you have good reason to, in response to changes in the real world environment. You will need to update your business plan from time to time to reflect substantial changes in strategy.

Each type of market area will require a different format of business plan. The outline which follows is a standard one that can be modified to be fit for purpose in your chosen field of operation. The following are key areas of the plan:

- **Executive summary** – this is an overview of the entire business plan, a summary written for people that can spend only a short time in understanding your business, but who will still gain a good knowledge of your business aims and objectives, how you structure your organization and the strategies you will use for success. It should be good enough to make investors feel confident about giving you a grant, loan, land or other vital resource.

- **Background** – a description of the vision statement (a long term goal stating where the company is going) and the mission statement (what the company is doing to achieve the vision). Here, you would describe how the idea for the business came about and justify its existence or provide rational reasons as to why and how you believe the enterprise will achieve its vision through its mission. Here is the opportunity to sell your business idea to potential partners, sources of finance or other resources and to anyone who represents a risk to your being able to become established. This includes government or financial regulators. A general statement of your risk management strategy will be required here.

Chapter 3   Nurturing Your Business Enterprise Idea

- **Description** of the business – detailed information on **what** your business will be doing for customers: what is the service? What is the product? What type of business status do you have and why? Examples of the latter include: sole trader, limited liability, partnership, limited liability partnership or public liability company. Further details may include a PESTEL analysis:

P-Political factors: This could influence the business e.g. a change of political party in government may affect the level of government subsidies and support.

E-Economic factors: This could influence the business, e.g. impact of global economic recession on available business funding.

S-Social factors: These are factors which can influence the development of the population and their ability to contribute to the economy and examples are; **education, health and with income distribution. Such factors will influence product or service marketing strategy or human resource management.**

T-Technology: These are factors that may influence the business marketing methods e.g. the recent changes in internet advertising standards and uptake of online marketing applications.

E-Environmental factors: These are those which influence the business. For example, the need to comply with eco-friendly operations in terms of your inputs or outputs, so as to meet statutory requirements and to appeal to clients.

L-Legal and governance issues: These are ones that are required to run the business. For example, the insurance policies used to protect your business from unforeseen circumstances. Also those required to show that your premises comply with fire, security, health and safety regulations.

It is here that one might also present the results of a SWOT analysis – S-strength, W-Weakness, O-Opportunities and T-Threats to the company. A further mention can be made here of the detailed breakdown of the risk assessment to operations and strategies to counter these risks.

- **Objectives** – A breakdown of the mission statement into detailed statements of how the mission statement is to be affected. The objectives should be S.M.A.R.T, to provide the basic framework for the operational structure of your business activities. There are a range of ways of presenting objectives to ensure they can be translated into the outputs delivered, inputs required and personnel desired to achieve success.

- **Marketing and Sales Strategy** – precise and detailed information which describes who you think your customers are going to be, where they located and how you are going to reach them. Basically, all the material

Chapter 3   Nurturing Your Business Enterprise Idea

that enables you to plan and implement an effective market strategy and monitor your performance.

- **Information on your management team and personnel** - the basic collection of facts concerning your labour requirements. This includes the qualifications, experience and achievements of staff needed to establish and maintain your business. In the plan you may wish to detail how you intend to source your staff and how to implement continuous professional development and motivation.

- **Management Information** - the knowledge base for the operation for your business. All the necessary facts upon which you operate your business premises, your information technology (IT) and client data confidentiality management, and your policies and procedures. This will include matters underlying your business attitudes, such as securing a triple bottom line: **those social, environmental and economic objectives which** add value to your business reputation.

- **Financial projections** - This is where you discuss your capital requirements in a manner that breaks it down into present and future requirements. This is where you state how much money or resources you need to start the business and where you are going to get these resources from. It has to answer the question, how much you think the business will make and over what time frame? Here the arrangement to manage money coming into your business (income) and money going out of your business (expenses) is also described.

Goal Setting and Goal Getting:

The principle of goal setting and reaching goals involves the making of clear daily, weekly, monthly or yearly objectives, preferably in writing, of what you need to attempt to achieve. It is all about creatively and consistently working to achieve these set goals in a timely and orderly manner. These goals could be as basic as making contact with your local council or contacting a business adviser to seek for help. If you fail to make this contact, you fail to set up the possibility of booking an appointment and getting the much needed support.

Goal setting involves breaking a goal into separate and distinct objectives, which then have to be described in such a way that they can be monitored using the SMART method, where:

S - Specific: State exactly what you aim to achieve
M - Measurable: Making reference to the units of output used in production
A - Achievable: Set objectives that are challenging but not impossible because they relate to the levels of input available

Chapter 3   Nurturing Your Business Enterprise Idea

***R** - Relevant: Make sure the set objectives are fulfilling your goals and meeting client expectations, adding value to your business*

***T** - Timely: Each objective needs to have dates associated with completion in order to check the process is on course and to take appropriate action for changes.*

Chapter 4

Winning Attitude

Chapter 4
Winning Attitude

Attitude determines Aptitude and Altitude

TO SUCCED IN YOUR BUSINESS ENTERPRISE, you need to have and maintain a winning business altitude, that is to say, level of performance. It will not only be up to your business beliefs and passions but also your mindset, your creative skills and how your inspire customers to trust your product and/or service. They also need to trust in the effects of your willingness to make yourself approachable and available for continuous, professional and social development (CPSD).

> *'In all you think and do, try operating within the borders of common sense, even though common sense appears to be no longer common.'*

The above are only some of the attitudes that make your service or product stand out for customers to notice and believe in, so as to spend their hard earned money purchasing.

Master how to give customers the conviction to use, buy or hire your services or your products repeatedly. University and academic qualifications alone may not guarantee your business success. Rather your academic, business *and* common sense knowledge of your market, *plus* your attitude to succeed, will sustain you en route to being successful.

My mother has a saying that is so special to her. She regularly states that **gaining an education does not mean gaining common sense**. In all you think and do in business and in your personal development, try operating within the borders of wisdom and common sense. This is true even though, it must be admitted, it appears that common sense is no longer as common as it used to be!

A winning attitude will support you to:

- Carry out market research in your selected business segment
- Write your business plan and continuously update it
- Attend business enterprise and personal development seminars that have impact on your business focus area
- Respond to the strengths of your competitors by becoming stronger
- Find out about and respond to your clients needs
- Improve where you and your competition are doing the same
- Take advantage of your competition's weaknesses.

Chapter 4   Winning Attitude

As a business trainer and management consultant, it is common to discuss and exchange information on incidents that have occurred during business training sessions. One of the most common incidents many trainers have experienced is that of meeting individuals who attend workshops with an un-teachable attitude. These individuals may have some knowledge of a particular business field and will prefer to interrupt and talk, rather than listen.

Back in high school, we used the term 'ITK: 'I Too Know,' to describe fellow students who have the similar attitude of claiming to know everything in class. Quite clearly, qualified and experienced trainers have skills and systems they can implement to keep such individuals inclusively engaged, happy and less disruptive. However, such attitudes can be a real pain and may affect further relationships between a business adviser and a business owner.

Such individuals could, on the other hand, be very passionate about their business idea. They may find it difficult to understand why they should go through business training exercises that will help them to transfer their business ideas from their head into their own, confidential, notebooks and to then take constructive actions to turn those business ideas into successful business enterprise.

Some of them may even refuse to take part in an exercise, not realising that it is important to liberate business ideas and processes trapped inside one's own head. When the ideas are transferred into other forms and acted upon constructively, it will speed up the process of bringing these ideas to life and to success.

Safe-guarding your business idea in this way is very important. So is having a character that allows you to be supported by experts; enables constructive criticism from friends and family and remains eager for continuous personal development.

> **A winning business attitude will give you a winning business aptitude, which will uphold a successful business altitude.**

Having a teachable spirit gives one a winning attitude, aptitude and therefore, altitude.

A winning business attitude will create a winning business aptitude, which will uphold a successful business altitude.

Starting and surviving in business has its challenges and will require you to work harder and smarter and even longer hours. Do not be deceived that becoming your own boss will make life immediately easier. In fact, it may actually make life tough for some time, though, if you are doing what you have passion and purpose for, you will love it the more.

Having your own business enterprise will definitely give you the flexibility to allow yourself more power to influence and manage your personal life better. This includes time for

Chapter 4   Winning Attitude

holidays, family, leisure, work and managing your income and expenses. Attending business enterprise and personal development workshops that will improve your knowledge, skills and enable you to network with other entrepreneurs is absolutely important. Though it is also critical that you also have the discipline to implement what you have learnt from these seminars.

Never allow past failures in business to scare you away from bouncing back and succeeding. Many successful business owners or entrepreneurs have a failed business in their past. A winning attitude will help you believe that you are the best in what you do and you will then carry out your business activities as 'the best', learning from 'the best' and hoping for 'the best'.

Failure can be a state of mind rather than a real event. Past business enterprise failures do not mean failure in your current business enterprise, rather it means that you are better experienced, operationally seasoned and enterprise refined to excel in your current and future business enterprise. Creatively use these lessons as the things which you have done in the past which, though they had little or no positive impact in the previous enterprise, may have a different effect now. This may be, simply because the experience of adversity can lead to advantage, through experience.

There is a rumour that many businesses will make losses in their first two years of operation and if you are very lucky you will break even in your first two years, before you can start making a profit. Do be careful of what you feed your mind, because people are making profit in their first year, let alone, first two years of business operation.

The question you need to ask yourself is this, 'what levels of business investment are you going to consider?'

You need to ascertain whether the amount of money required to start trading is high, medium or low. Is it a few thousand, million or billion pounds (£), dollars ($), naira (₦) or rand (R)? Some investment levels may require more strategic planning, operations and time to bring you profit.

If you have the mindset that this 'failure rumour' will apply to your enterprise, that you may require a few thousand or a few hundreds of unit capital just to keep running, then you are attracting this same failure to you, as the *law of attraction* states.

> **'Past business failure, does not mean failure in your current business; rather it means you are better experienced, operationally seasoned and enterprise refined to excel in your current enterprise, because adversity can lead to advantage.'**

This rumour insists that the first one or

Chapter 4   Winning Attitude

two years in business will naturally have some challenges, just like the first one or two years in a new country or new career will have challenges. However, you *can* make profits, not just in your first two years, but even in your first year.

Some helpful winning attitudes are:

- Spend your money and resources wisely and creatively
- Maintain accurate records of income and expenses
- Manage your business customers fairly as they are the indirect owners of your business
- Choose and register the right business form, at the right time, with the right government agency

'If you have the mindset that your business will make losses or only break even in the first two years of operation, then you are inviting this law of attraction to apply to your business, in this way.'

- Open the right business bank account
- Avoid mixing personal money and business money
- Under-promise your clients and then over-deliver
- Work hard and, most importantly, work smart
- Understand what your competition is doing

- Believe in your service and products and remain teachable
- Keep the taxman, bank manager and your customers happy

If you lose money at the end of your first one or two years in business, you are not alone. When you break even at the end of your first one or two years in business, you are doing well. If you make profit at the end of the first one or two years in business, you are proving your altitude. Celebrate it and then, get back to work!

Chapter 5

Personal Development

Chapter 5

Personal Development

The Balance between Possibility and Impossibility

SUCCEEDING IN A COMPETITIVE BUSINESS ARENA requires competitive skills, competitive advantage and continuous professional development. The economic gap between the rich and the poor keeps widening; the poor are getting poorer and the rich are getting richer. One of the reasons for this is because the rich keep doing what they have been doing and are becoming richer and the poor keep doing what they have been doing and are becoming poorer.

The difference between the rich and the poor has a lot to do with how **informed** the rich and the poor are; their **ability** and **willingness to improve their situation** and how **disciplined** they are **towards their personal and professional development**.

During one of my training workshops, an icebreaker was introduced, as an exercise to make everyone comfortable and alert to best engage with the training.

Chapter 5 Personal Development

A question was directed at the audience to think, write down and then give an oral presentation of what success means to them and the impact this would have on their personal development.

The responses received from the audience were interesting, and what follows are a few of these responses:

- Success means finding and fulfilling life destiny
- Success is having a health and wealthy life
- Success is when you choose to live life and refuse that life lives you
- Success is when the sky is no longer your limit but the starting point
- Success is attaining a balance in every aspect of your life

One person also stated that through personal development he had learned one of the secrets of what lies between the poor and the rich. As a life coach, I immediately understood that the other people attending my training seminar would benefit if they understood exactly what this secret was. I also believe in inclusive learning, so I engaged the gentleman further and asked him what he felt the specific secret was.

'Some people live life, while others allow life to live them. You are created to be the best, accept to live life and reject life living you'.

He stated that one distinctive difference between the reasoning of the poor and the rich is that when the poor make, or acquire, a lump sum of money, the majority of them will just spend, spend and spend the money and then, just as the money is finishing, they will start looking for where to invest the remaining money.

On the other hand the majority of rich people when they make, or acquire, a lump sum of money will just invest, invest and invest the money in businesses that make profit and then, with what is remaining they will spend.

What the word success means to **you** is a question that you need to answer for yourself, mentally and then write down, memorise and save, because that is a core value of your life. Your Success Core Value (SCV) is equal to Identify It (II) plus Write It (WI) multiplied by Do It Right (DIR).

$$SCV = II + WI \times DIR$$

'A difference between the rich and the poor is this: when the poor receives a large lump sum of money they spend widely and then invest what remains when the money is about to finish but the rich invest first and spend what remains.'

Remember that it's only through such logical thinking and written affirmation that great men and women of current and past generations

Chapter 5   Personal Development

such as: Nelson Mandela, Moliere, Abraham Lincoln, Maya Angelou, Desmond Tutu, and Mother Theresa etc., spoke words which become highly quoted. So much so, that we still identify with them until today.

'Never focus on what you have lost in the past. Acknowledge what you have now because the past will never come back and sometimes the future may give you back what you have lost in the past, better

Once you have written down what success means to you, print it out in any format that appeals to you and laminate or frame it and then display it somewhere you can read it every day.

It then becomes a monumental inspiration that comes from your own thoughts and your own belief in what success means to you. This will motivate you to be in touch with your core passion and perfect purpose and to go on to be the best you deserve to be in your life.

Remember, success may mean only one thing to you but it may also mean more than one thing to you. Acknowledge this meaning, accept that plans need to be made to fulfil it and take the actions that are required to make it happen, do this again and again until it becomes part of your nature.

To reinforce the idea about affirmation and belief, I recall a tale I heard whilst enjoying listening to BBC Radio Four. During one of their programmes there was a story told of a mother and her two daughters who shared an idea which they practiced. The three ladies lived in a part of town where car parking was pretty difficult to find but they owned a car. They developed a mindset that whenever they needed to secure a parking place for their car, they would. So each time, as they drove home whilst approaching, they would start singing a rhyme they had made up. The basic message of the rhyme was to ask what they called their 'Parking Angel' to provide a parking space for their car. The majority of their 'requests' were granted, and they secured a space. Not all the time but certainly for most of the time. The ladies actually started arguing about the gender of their parking angel!

It matters little if you were **born** rich or poor, what matters more is that you know that you have a right to develop yourself and be better than how you were born in the way you see fit. You have a right to develop your business enterprise ideas to become attractive and marketable enough for you to succeed.

The above tale might sound like a fairy tale. However, the real tale is for you to learn the need to develop a mindset to believe in yourself and in your business idea(s) and in the service or products your business delivers or produces.

Chapter 5   Personal Development

Choose to call it the 'law of the universe' or whatever you might like to call it. The simple issue here is, 'if you keep doing what you have always done, you will always get what you have always had.' In order to achieve something that you never possessed before, you have to do something you have never done before.

Many individual(s) allow their lack of positive mindset or self-belief to keep them in employment which they are not happy in or which they know is not their true career path.

Managing the power of fear (false evidence appearing real) and laziness (lack of action, zeal intelligence and negative excuses), is what will help you *unleash your life's greatness*. Search for a career where your passion and perfect purpose lies is the true way to succeed.

'If you keep doing what you have always done, you will always get what you have always had and to get something that you never had before, you have to do something

Staying in jobs or careers which are unsuited to the true you for too long, or even for the entirety of your productive life will bring about only passive growth and a sense of disappointment in yourself. Finding a career or enterprise that ignites your passion and which is drawn from your perfect purpose could be one of your

- 55 -

biggest challenges in life. When you do find it, you will be on your way to the top.

Remember, though, you cannot find it if you don't look for it! You may make mistakes, you may hurt yourself and even hurt others whilst en route, these things are human, but once you have found your purpose and passion, you are forever financially, and in many other ways, free.

The possibility of disappointment in business relationships and transactions is great. It is not **if** **it will** happen, but rather, **when** **it will** happen. Learn from your mistakes, learn to endure, learn to forgive and learn to move forward. Forgiveness is not only for the person or persons who may have hurt you in business, but also for you, to be able to move on. The above is a positive learning tool to help you to move on into your successful career: better, safer, quicker and wiser.

Refuse to only focus on what you have lost in the past in business. Constantly assess what it is that you have now. The past will never return and in many cases the future can bring to you what you have lost in the past: better, bigger and more beautiful than before.

Remember, when you are down, have no fear because any change in your enterprise situation must be upwards. So arise and ***unleash your life's greatness.***

Chapter 6

Choosing Business Location

Chapter 6
Choosing Business Location

It's all in the presentation

LOCATING A NEW BUSINESS OR RELOCATING AN EXISTING BUSINESS has challenges. A business premises is not exactly the same as a business location, though it sounds similar.

The business location is a geographical choice of whether to locate your business in the east, south, west or north or perhaps even in the centre of a city like London, Lagos, Laos, Limpopo or Los Angeles.

Business premises on the other hand, specifically responds to the question of: what type of office or factory premises you need for your business, now that you have chosen a geographical location.

It is important that you can understand the difference between the words: 'want and need,' in business. A 'want' is something you would like to have that is not a necessity and you can do without at that particular moment in time. You may feel better having it, as in the case of a cable television subscription or an extra pair of black shoes because it is on sale.

Chapter 6 Choosing Business Location

On the other hand a 'need' could be a problem that you need to solve, for example, paying your mortgage, business premise rent or your house rent, which, if you don't pay might result in you having no shelter over your head, that of your office as well as that of your family.

When choosing a business location and premises, it is important to take into consideration factors such as:

> **'A 'Want' is an item you can do without having at that particular moment in time such as buying an extra pair of black shoes just because it is on sale. A 'Need' is paying your house rent as if you don't pay, could mean no shelter for your family.'**

- Cost – Can you afford it for at least the next one to two years and maintain a competitive edge compared to rivals?
- Proximity to target customers – is it easy to locate and travel to and accessible to all your customers?
- Proximity to suppliers – Is it easy to locate and accessible to your suppliers?

- Safety and security – are you and your staff and resources safe?
- Proximity to a bank – is there banking accessibility when required?
-

Consider choosing to either start your business from home or renting or hiring a business premises depending upon:
- The type of business you are setting up - A web designer can start-up from home with less challenges than a restaurant business
- Are there legal constraints? – Check your tenancy and mortgage agreement to see if there are clauses in support or against setting up a business from home
- Will working from home influence your performance negatively, or inspire you to be more active and professional with your business enterprise?
- How disciplined are you to trade from home and, at the same time, keeping and respecting all professional office principles as applicable?

If you start your business from home it can save you initial cash expenses. This can give you the ability to use your money to deal with other expenses. If this is your choice, then you need to dedicate a space in your home as your business premises office. This is a requirement of the tax office to allow you claim financial considerations on utility bills, etc. This could be a simple, office table and chair, together with what you need

Chapter 6   Choosing Business Location

for your business: personal computer, office electronic gadgets, stationery and files depending on your actual business operations.

This home space must operate with a professional office culture as if you were in a business premises outside of your home. It should be a space where clients can come into the office at any time and not find you relaxing informally. Your clients should not find you eating your lunch on your office table, with an overspill on top of your business documents and files!

The idea behind dressing formally to work in a home office, just like you'll dress to work from a public located office is that it brings a positive impact on your work output.

Once you have setup your home office, have a memory of your designated space e.g. the square that makes up your home office inside, for example your bedroom. Before you step into that home office space, it is an idea to dress as if you are going to an office located in a public business premises.

The idea behind dressing formally to work from a home office is that there can be a positive influence on your work output. I have, in reality, seen people who work from a home office in their bedroom, kitchen, dining room, sitting room or other part of their house. They will dress up as if going to an office located outside their house. They will leave home, lock their front door, walk around their building block and then come back into their house to start work. These businessmen and women believe it brings their mindset in tune to an office environment, helps them become focused and so their work output is higher, better and stronger.

One of my first business enterprise mentors was Brian Smith of **Simple Business Solutions**. He once said to me, "The more professional that you look while operating from your home office, the more professional your work output will appear to stakeholders i.e. clients, competitors and suppliers etc."

If you step into your home office in pyjamas with a hot plate of pizza and a hot cup of tea, your work output will reflect this with debris of pizza and droplet of tea all over the table and perhaps on some important documents. This is not good for your personal, professional and business reputation.

Here is a tip concerning the choice of a cost effective way to start your business, though it depends on the type of business operations you have. Some service focused business operations may require, and thus enable, you to use the clients' offices to deliver your services to them. Such service providers include trainers, counsellors, therapists, coaches and psychologists. While working with Life coaches, business trainers and advisers, I often use clients' office premises to deliver ninety-

Chapter 6   Choosing Business Location

percent of my business trainings, which saves me the cost of hiring training rooms.

Clients often book an appointment with me to deliver business development training; one-to-one coaching management consultation and research, development and business strategy sessions. They are often happy for me to come and use their office premises or training rooms. This is because most of the processes, issues and documents under discussion may be located at the client's location and it reduces the cost, for clients travelling to an external venue, outside of the workplace, for consultation or training.

There are some business activities that will definitely be required, by government regulation, for certain operations to be carried out outside of your home environment due to issues of fire, health and safety. The best way you can be sure if you can trade from home, initially, is to make an appointment to speak to a business adviser who will discuss your particular circumstances. They will explore your rental agreement, mortgage contract and

If you step into your home office in pyjamas with hot plate of pizza and cup of tea, your work output will reflect this with debris of pizza and droplets of tea all over the table and on some important documents.

business operation as well as government regulations that may or may not apply to you.

Where there are questions that cannot be answered, an experienced business adviser has networks of other business advisers, consultants and commercial experts to signpost you to get more and relevant support.

Chapter 7

Sourcing Start-Up Funds

Chapter 7

Sourcing Start-Up Funds

The Lubricating Oil of Business Enterprise

THE FULL LUBRICATION OF YOUR ENTERPRISE will require some initial funding. How to plan and structure this process is essential, as failure to plan is planning to fail. Sourcing your business start-up fund is very likely one of the major factors that scare away many people from starting their own business.

If you are a first timer in business, you might find it very challenging to come to terms with how to raise initial start-up funds. The fear of this could cause you to believe that being an employee is the best and most feasible choice for you. The choice you make between staying as an employee and becoming self-employed, and potentially an employer, is the same choice to be made between receiving 'salary' and making 'profit.' It is your choice to choose to make profit or receive salary. The sooner you consider wisely and make an informed choice, the better. It is important to realise that who you are currently working for had to figure out a way to resolve this choice, this challenge, to be able to employ and pay you and make a profit instead of receiving wages or salary.

Chapter 7   Sourcing Start-Up Funds

I have learnt that there are three kinds of people in life: those who make things happen, those who observe things happen and those who have no clue as to what is going on. Which one of these are you?

> **'There are three kinds of people in life: those who make things happen, those who observe things happen and those who have not got a clue as to what is going on.'**

When you have a business idea and have developed the business awareness to transform your idea into reality, a good potential source of finance can be a huge challenge but it should not be your final 'bus stop' to give up.

Firstly, a thorough look into your type of business will help you understand what quantity of funds you may initially require. Then, plan how to go about exploring, identifying and applying for appropriate fund options.

All types of business require initial funding; though service delivery based businesses may allow you more flexibility, when compared to product based business. The latter may require purchase or hire of cash-intensive machinery from the beginning.

There are over fifty businesses that you can start with less than £1,000 and some of them include:

Caterer, Child minder, Book-keeper, Carpenter, Painter, Decorator, Children's Entertainer, Computer Maintenance, DJ, Editor Face Painter, Personal Shopper, Make Up Artist, Natural Cosmetics Maker, Florist, Gardener, Aromatherapist, Interpreter, Dance Instructor, Private Tutor, Events Organizer, Party Planner, Domestic Engineer, Handy Man, Graphic Designer, Ironing Service, Marketing Consultant, Personal Stylist, Photographer, Music Instructor, Fine Artist, Contemporary Artist, Jewelry Designer, Security Service, Plumber, Sculptor, Martial Arts Coach, Massage therapist, Nail Technician, Wedding Planner, Fashion Designer, Music Promoter, Nutritionist, Herbal Therapist, Fitness Trainer, Personal Trainer, Life Coach, Virtual Assistant, Dog Walker, Vocal Coach, Freelance Hair Dresser, Web Designer, Cake Decorator, Consultant, Potter, Book Editor

Chapter 7   Sourcing Start-Up Funds

At a personal coaching course I once attended, I met a lady who was a qualified counsellor and was attending the course to also become a qualified life and personal coach. During the numerous interactive exercises at the training course we were asked to use some of the methods that we were taught to support and motivate our clients without advising our clients. It is better to use the tools to support their transformation from where they are at present to where they need to be, faster, safer and wiser than if they were to do it by themselves.

> *'In business you must either love or respect the tax man and the bank manager. Never allow the tax man to even think of re-checking your records and never allow the trust which the bank manager has in you to be questioned.'*

By supporting the client to realise their strengths and their own creative solutions and strategies they will be inspired to positively move on with their life aspirations.

The lady I met mentioned that she was interested in starting up her own business, but had many concerns as to how to raise the initial capital to start-up.

I asked her what she exactly needed the capital to do, if the capital was her only challenge, since she possessed the knowledge and skills needed to set up a counselling and coaching service.

She responded that she needed the money to rent an office space and buy office equipment. I then asked her if she need to immediately start from a rented office. She responded of her awareness that some organisations, such as hospitals, prisons and education institutions prefer to have counsellors come in and use their own offices for consultations.

She was amazed at that idea and mentioned noticing external counsellors come from outside to use the consultation rooms of her present employer but she had not thought about it in that way. At that point, she had a flash bulb moment in her mind. She saw that there was an alternative to the funding issue that had been her barrier to starting her business. She opened up to her realisation that these other external counsellors were actually presenting a solution to what she thought was a barrier to starting up.

She has since, started her own business from home and delivering counselling service, plus her newly acquired life and personal coaching skills, to hospitals, care homes and higher education institutions, prisons around London using these latter organisations' premises.

In the UK the tax office actually allows you to claim about £165 per year as expenses for working from your home. It will be

Chapter 7   Sourcing Start-Up Funds

worthwhile checking what is available, in this respect, in your country of business.

This may well compensate for electricity and heating costs. The amount is usually calculated without verification or asking any questions. Anything above that amount, they may require verification and further questions may be asked by the tax office. Also if you use your personal home phone to make business calls, it may be required of you to prove the percentage of personal calls and business calls you make. You will need to use a combination of itemised phone bills and a listing of your work numbers. So, if you claim to be making forty percent business calls and sixty percent personal calls from your phone each year, you can include 40% of your phone calls as business expenses, during your annual tax returns.

After a year this lady, who had now become a business associate, rang me to thank me for my support. I asked her what her business unique selling point (USP) was. She responded that it was,' the ability to serve clients using counselling and coaching methods supportive of both males and females to deal with past, present and future issues, by helping them activate their dormant mental and personal strengths'.

So I put the same question to you: what is the unique selling point of your business?

There are many business enterprises you can start with the knowledge and skills you have accumulated in life or at work with £1000 (Great Britain Pound), $100 (United States Dollar) and R1000 (South African Rand) and so on. Do not use the lack of money as an adversary to your business enterprise start-up. Rather, activate the money you have to your advantage.

Wealthy people have a mindset which operates at the frequency of success. So learn to transform your mindset to operate in the same frequency with regards to money. Success will be attracted to you and money will work for you. Learn to stop limiting yourself by the financial aspects of important training, idea promotion and investments that will positively impact upon your life. Rather, explore the value that training or investment will add to you to **unleash your life's greatness**.

Remember the principle of cause and effect which states that; your positive actions are effects which are accounted for by reasons which are the causes as to why these effects take place. This also happens in reverse, where you supply excuses as to why you were unable to take positive actions. Many people intentionally or unintentionally allow themselves to be self-sabotaged by this reasoning. Whereas, in reality, the solutions may be there, present, right in their face. The solutions may be there in the home, work place, social organisation, community, religious organisation and so on. Open your eyes to observe the solution. Plan and **unleash your life's greatness**.

Raising money to start your business enterprise is more achievable if you can make the little money you already have

Chapter 7   Sourcing Start-Up Funds

go a long way. This money has to work and serve you; it is not for you to work to serve the money.

There is an old tool of commerce called 'bartering'. In bartering you can use your goods or skills, in trade, to gain materials, skills and services of another person without the need of a physical money transaction. Rather, the exchange of materials and or services is the transactional obligation. I shall give an example below as how one can use the bartering concept offectively in business to save money.

At one of my training workshops on the power of effective networking, I encouraged and taught the participants how to dress to impress and, importantly, how to network to genuinely connect with strangers and potential clients at network events.

I then asked them to use the training as a practical tool to assist them to perform a real networking exercise. Using the bartering method, I asked them to use their own skills to seek for another service, as the skill of an entrepreneur, who is looking for the skill they were offering.

One young man who operates a restaurant business and who was looking for an accountant to manage his tax returns used his powers of negotiation and bartering to resolve his needs.

The accountant he had identified had just started his business, after qualifying, and was located close to his restaurant.

They identified their needs and negotiated a fair and equitable exchange of them.

What bartering effectively did for them was to save both of them from spending their limited supply of physical cash. Rather than achieving their business needs through financial payment for the rendering of an accounting service to the restaurant, the restaurant owner provided, to the accountant, during office-hours, meals. This was agreed for a specified period of time and in ways that both parties believed to be fair. For both of them, this added value to their respective business needs.

'Bartering uses your skills to render service and gain the skills of another person's service with no need for physical money transaction; rather the exchange of services is the transaction.'

When you apply such networking, business and entrepreneurial skills you can effectively reduce, manage and control the spending of your limited finances. This will enable your cash to go further so you can purchase those services for which you may not be able to barter. The services received through bartering will equally go a long way in adding value and profit to your business.

Creative thinking, positioning, prospecting, factoring and planning are recognised tools in business which are suggested to assist you to think outside the box when looking for new clients and dealing with money matters. When you are in a situation where initial business start-up finance is a make or break issue, think of employing the above tools.

Another avenue to explore in raising funds is using your enterprise skills to deliver critical or needed services to your local council, charity, church and community.

Think of the idea of delivering voluntary services to the above organisations. Also, consider doing an internship in an organisation which is already established and which is in the same kind of enterprise in which you intend to start your business. Such internships and voluntary charity service delivery with local councils, charity, community, church organisations, schools, hospitals and private corporate organisations can be viewed as strong networking tools. This activity may play a pivotal role in attracting new finances into your business sooner than you think. Insofar as you have served competently and kept positive contact with people who have the will, ability and authority to use and authorise payment for your business service in the future, you will have built up for yourself a useful network of potential clients. Connecting to the less powerful people in authority is important but may not be as useful as connecting with the individuals that control the corridors of power in these organisations, so consider your contacts wisely!

Creating new contacts and making new connections in your

business environment can be a valuable tool that may expose you to the advantages of new or existing funding opportunities that you may be able to secure.

> *'Business Knowledge gives power in the mind of a successful entrepreneur and it is even more powerful if used wisely.'*

This is the reason for my appreciation of the statement that 'business knowledge is power' in the mind of an entrepreneur. It is even more powerful if used wisely. This is so true and I believe that every business person has to understand and know the strong distinctions between:

- What you think you know
- What you don't know that you know
- What you know that you don't know
- What you don't know that you don't know

The entrepreneur's brain can be viewed as having these distinctive modes of perception which reflect the four ideas above.

It is only through knowledge, interaction and by engaging with great minds that you can actively and purposefully stimulate your brain cells to become more alert to areas that will support your development.

Chapter 7   Sourcing Start-Up Funds

'I see NLP, Neuron Linguistic Programming, as a method that activates my brain to explore new platforms; exposes me to ways to manage and enhance my creative concepts and encourages my eyes to see and to use new avenues to create multiple streams of success in my life.'

When you don't use some of the skills that you possess for a long period of time, your brain will, as a consequence, programme itself in such a way that these skills become inactive. Your brain will deactivate the use of those skills until you activate those skills again or else they stay asleep for your lifetime and so may forever be lost to the possibility of you **unleashing your life's greatness**.

Another example is, if, and when, you stop using and speaking a certain language you have learnt how to speak or you have understood, for a very long period of time, you may notice that your skill in that language will weaken. Once you find yourself in an environment where you start speaking the language again, after a period of time, your command and skill in that particular language will start coming back to you.

I view the Neuron linguistic Program (NLP) as an enterprise tool and method. It can help you activate your brain to explore new business platforms and to create new sources of finance. It does this by exposing you to ways of managing your current finances better and enhances your thinking with new concepts of creating finance and sales and encourages you to continuously keep your eyes open to see and to utilize new ways of succeeding.

Personally, I love delivering voluntary services to my local community, whether national or global. These services might be referred to as an internship or voluntary work, but it really opens doors of opportunities into organisations. Importantly, you must know what you are looking for so when it turns up, or you discover it, you understand how to grab hold of it so as to use it positively, correctly and wisely.

It was during one such voluntary internship programme within a business advisory, training and management consultancy that I finally found my life's passion and perfect purpose. Although I had an interest in this field for years, during that internship it became crystal clear to me that it was my calling. This is who I am and what I do today and I am still researching and claiming my long term vision in business consultancy. I have always known that I would gain great satisfaction from what I do now: positively provoking thoughts, impacting lives and transforming people to be the best they can be in their career, profession and business life. I have also known that I would love putting a smile on another person's face through my work. I have always known that my skills would help transform ordinary processes

Chapter 7   Sourcing Start-Up Funds

to extraordinary systems; change ineffective ways into effective, successful and sustainable schemes with immeasurable benefits.

Today, I look back and relish taking that voluntary internship.

Though it only paid for my lunch each day and that was all I received for the duration of my internship, the benefits today are immeasurable and will remain so.

> **'I love voluntary service to my community and society. Call it internship or selfless service, but it really opens opportunities for you. You must know what you're looking for so that when it turns up, you can grab it and use it wisely.'**

My mentor during this voluntary internship period exposed me to recognising an attitude that works both as a strength and weakness, for and against me.

It is my perfectionist attitude to producing systems which work precisely and accurately and which are consistently good in delivering high quality services.

My perfectionist attitude may not be so good for timely delivery of services and therefore, it may delay gaining an income from the payment for that service. This is because money coming into your business is an invaluable business survival instrument and should not be delayed on account of a perfectionist mindset. By trying to get every single product and service right, as well as the processes used to produce them to be perfect, delays will occur. This means your business will become known for a delayed service and/or product delivery.

On the strength side, my dedicated internship mentor exposed me to the idea that getting your service and product to always meet the customers need, is a must. This does not need to delay your business delivery activities, your customer loyalty and therefore your business income.

May be it is time you ask yourself if you are a perfectionist?

Perfectionists' ability to get systems work precisely and perfectly can be used at those crunch moments when and where perfection is required to serve your business vision (dream, goals and expectation) and mission statements (steps you need to take to achieve your dream).

However, this perfection should not be at the cost of disadvantage to service delivery time or else you may not meet your customer's own business demands and needs.

Wasting time will cost you money, lose you money, create unhappy customers and give your competition an opportunity to slip in unnoticed.

It is definitely a true statement, in business, that 'Time is Money'. In just the same way a positive, effective and timely presentation leads to customer conviction. The more your customers are happy speaking to you, the less they will speak to your business competition.

Be encouraged to share in the pride of acknowledging the power and potential of volunteering and use your enterprise skills to do voluntary activities and internship programmes to practically learn business skills that give you the following:

'Your business services and products must always meet the customers need but this does not necessarily need to delay your business delivery time, customer loyalty and business income. Maybe it's time you ask yourself: Are you are a perfectionist?'

- Master how to make little money go a long way and so act like big money
- Learn that good business entrepreneurs should not only thrive in good business seasons, but are resilient, able to survive bad business seasons as well
- Find a great mentor who is always there for you and willing to share knowledge
- Find and do something about your perfect enterprise purpose, your career purpose and the character of your successful business

You can achieve all these for your business enterprise if you understand your goal, commitment and purpose. You also must understand the impact of failure and impact of success upon yourself. It will be useful to understand your personal barriers to achievement; how much control do you have over these goals? What is your mindset towards these things and what time is available to achieve these goals?

The people you meet and mix with and the way you see yourself can positively influence or negatively influence your mindset when you start and are surviving in the business world.

I remember the story of an elephant that looked at itself in a mirror and saw the image of an ant, whilst at the same time, a mouse looked at itself in a mirror and saw an image of a lion, the 'king of the jungle'. How do you see yourself?

> *'An elephant looked at itself in a mirror and saw the image of an ant, whilst a mouse looked at itself in a mirror and saw an image of a lion, the 'king of the jungle'. How do you see yourself?'*

It is not only about how you see yourself but also about what you can do with this self concept. These thoughts impact upon how you relate to your target customer and contacts and this, in turn, impacts upon how these contacts will make your business name be heard widely, especially in the corridors of power. Some people refer to this as having good connections, while others may refer to it as having 'ways and means'. The fact is you need to thrive in this way to succeed in your business enterprise to **unleash your life's greatness.**

Family and friends can be another source of funding. Remember, however, it is not every friend that understands the importance of starting your own business and many of them will discourage you. This may not be because they don't want you to progress; rather they indirectly or directly discourage you because they don't understand. Also, their career mindset may be at the level of employee, rather than employer, which may influence you because they may lack the tenacity, foresight and knowledge to be the best they can to **unleash their life's greatness.**

This is not to encourage you to avoid such people, but be expectant to be cautious of them. Be mindful of what you say to them and speak less of your ideas around them, if you cannot avoid them.

The more you talk about your unique ideas to those who are stagnant as far as their creativity is concerned, the more they will argue with you and dampen your enterprise energy and may even kill it. However that is only possible, if you allow them to destroy it. **You** have the ultimate influence and **you** are in control of what anyone can damage in your 'enterprise mind.' Some of these issues may delay you from reaching your enterprise goals, but you will never be denied reaching your success, if you choose for it not to be denied.

All the same, your friends and family can be a good source of financial support if and when you need the funds to start your business enterprise. Should you be so blessed to have such friends and family willing to give you such money without asking for interest payment, then do use that opportunity now, rather than later. Be prudent and pay back the money when it is due. In this way you will not block such goodwill measures for others and future entrepreneurs that will need the same kind of initial business start-up financial support.

'Friends may or may not discourage you not because they don't want you to progress; rather they discourage you because they don't understand. They have a mindset of an employee; they lack the tenacity, foresight and knowledge to be successful in business enterprise.'

In some cultures, it is understood that during a wedding, the newly-weds are given a lump sum of money, as gifts, by friends and families. These friends and family may come together as a finance group to raise these funds and donate to the newly wedded couple.

Chapter 7   Sourcing Start-Up Funds

This funding can be used by the couple to offset their marriage expenses or even set up their business. If this applies to you, please use this sum wisely and profitably because it is a great source of initial business start-up money.

Banks definitely play good roles in raising cash for the property business and for very large businesses. It is imperative you compare different loan rates. Be careful with what you sign, checking for clauses that may tie you into debt forever.

I had a personal experience of a business owner who used his life savings and money from friends and family to start a restaurant business. For him, it meant he has to prepare food within the premises. A local authority regulation demands that the owner of a restaurant have an A3 license, which allows food to be prepared within, and then sold on the premises.

The gentleman rented a business premises and signed a 15-year tenancy contract without any break-away clause. Only afterwards did he think to enquire from the council about his license and found that he could not prepare food inside the premises because it was of A2 class, which does not allow for food preparation within. This was tough for him to manage because he had a 15 years tenancy and could not terminate it without serious financial loss and cannot deliver his business plan. This is one example as to why you will always be better off speaking to a business adviser before you sign any tenancy agreement or even before you send off your business registration form to register a business name. Consult a business adviser also before you choose a legal form of business e.g. sole trader, limited liability Company or partnership, etc.

A good business adviser will have contacts with solicitors, estate agents and accountants that are prudent and actively registered with the Law Society, Chartered Institute of Management Accountants and the Association of Chartered ACCA and Certified Accountants CIMA. Check their websites thoroughly and/or contact these regulators to know if the accountant or solicitor you may be thinking of using are

> ***'Any solicitor, accountant and adviser who carelessly allows documents to lie all over their office, will some day be careless with your documents leading to lost or defaced documents due to poor office and document management.'***

registered active members. If you use an accountant or solicitor who is correctly regulated, should you need to seek compensation or appropriate punitive action, these regulators will assist you in cases of unprofessional service providers whose work has had an adverse effect on your business.

When you need an accountant or solicitor for your business, please visit their offices and chambers and speak to them face to face. Pay attention to the way the office is managed, notice

Chapter 7   Sourcing Start-Up Funds

if documents are tidy or untidy, check if documents are carefully filed or are randomly tied up and packed carelessly under tables and on shelves etc.

The truth of the matter is that any solicitor, business adviser, accountant or professional who is to support your business, who allows you to witness carelessly placed documents all over their office, will someday allow your own documents to be carelessly placed, which could lead to lost or defaced documents and exposure of your confidential information to competitors. This is due to poor office and document management and could lead to a breach of client's Data Protection Act 1998.

When and if you find such signs, please excuse yourself politely and think again. Do you want to do business and give your money to such people? If you need quality service, count your losses quickly and check elsewhere.

Chapter 8

Marketing Your Business

Chapter 8

Marketing Your Business

Customer's Conviction is Key to Success

CONVINCING CUSTOMERS TO USE YOUR SERVICES AND PRODUCTS requires a refined promotion and advertising process that assists prospective customers to answer any of their questions or concerns about your product and/or service. At this point, you would have developed your business enterprise's unique selling points and be conveying this message in a manner and a language that your target customers understand. By now you should have written down your business plan and used it to clearly establish that you know what gaps exist in terms of opportunities in your market. This will be used to assure customers that your services and products can economically and 'ecologically' fill these gaps and add value. Your purpose is to assure and meet the needs of all stakeholders such as: suppliers, customers, the tax office, the bank manager and the array of relevant government legislations e.g. fire, food safety, health and safety and so on.

Marketing does not necessarily need to use all your business finance. It is important you find the most cost-effective way to reach your target customers and convince them that you have the goods or services they need, through using economic and innovative marketing, advertising, promotion and sale methods.

You should already know who your competitors are through market research. Market research can either be primary or secondary research. Secondary research includes typing your business sector on web search engines and then exploring what it is they are doing, according to a range of pre-set consideration. You can also do this by relying on research findings carried out by trusted organisations like the government departments of commerce, business and innovation and by recognised peer research that has been carried out by public or private organisations.

Alternatively, you could achieve this through primary research, where you personally design and implement questionnaires by carrying out surveys and making telephone calls or administering them to selected groups who may be friends, family and associates. However, if you have already ascertained who your target market is, it would be better to use a selected sample group to whom you will ask questions. This group of people will be asked to answer pre-designed, open-ended questions which allow a better response to your research. These will provide more details than closed-ended questions, which only require a 'yes' or 'no'. The latter lacks depth which you will later find to be of great significance to your research findings.

Chapter 9   Your Business Starts Trading

With your research output it is important that they are processed adequately, so they can be used by you to be able to respond to your business domain using the following research response model:

- What your competitors do better (You should RESPOND)
- What your competitors do worse (You should EXPLOIT)
- What your competitors do same with you (You should IMPROVE)

Practising the above effectively will help solve particular problems or fill particular gaps and so enhance clients' satisfaction through receiving greater value for money.

Consider the following. If your competitor has been in a particular business location for more years than you have, it may have enabled them to have acquired loyalty from local customers. Through your in-depth research, you may have observed for example, that they open by 7 am and close by 7 pm. Now, using this information and creative thinking, you might wish to ask yourself, how can you open by 12:00 noon, rather than 7:00 am, as your competition already does and close by 12:00 midnight, rather than 7:00 pm, as your competition does?

This might have the effect of increasing sales, by out-manoeuvring the established competitor, especially during the evening hours after 7 pm. It will also allow you time to do banking activities and other business creative planning during the morning hours and it will enable you to operate at a time where there is no competition from your rival firm and so help you to generate a new set of loyal, after 7 pm customers when your competition is closed.

This is an idea that could be applied, dependent upon the type of business you run and your client's needs for your service at certain hours of the day. Customers who need to make purchases after 7:00pm could become loyal to your ability to make provisions at that time and could, therefore, become repeat customers. You would be in a better position to develop new marketing promotions that give special deals to these new customers. They can use these to invite or inform their friends, associates and family members about the late evening services which add value to their needs.

The whole idea is to use research to innovatively or creatively find gaps that you can explore to increase your customer base.

The case for starting your business enterprise needs to be creative, strategic, practical, exciting and, most importantly, structured to solve and improve specific need(s) of your target customers at a specific economic cost.

Let us look at the issue of setting a price for your services and/or products. Many new businesses, when asked how much their services cost, find it difficult to give straight and direct answers. A good example of this is responding to the question, 'how much does your service or goods cost?' A good entrepreneur may choose to state, 'Prices start from £20 and go up to £200.' The 'from' specifies the minimum price/charge for your service or goods, and not the maximum. An example can be seen with tour and holiday companies and airlines, who will state on their website that flight tickets start **'from'** £197.

A further example is the way in which they promote their service charges. A business service may offer what is known as 'Attractive Pricing', where they give clients, for example, seven hours service for the price of six hours. In this way, it will cost clients £600 instead of £700 and thus save them £100.

> **'Learn what your competitors do better than you (Then RESPOND).**
> **Learn what they are doing worse than you (Then EXPLOIT it).**
> **Learn what they are doing the same as you (Then, IMPROVE upon it).'**

This pricing may go on to attract further customers, thereby increasing overall profits. The point of this is that you can be specific, flexible and attractive in your business pricing. However, it is important to remember that in business, 'no deal' is better than 'bad deal'. This simply means, if you cannot negotiate a good price to sell your service or product to a customer, you are better off not making a sale, rather than making bad sale, which either is under priced or over-priced. This sets up a poor promotion image to your potential clients.

Marketing has a lot to do with verbal communication. It is important for you to design and master your business mission and vision statement. In my business, the following mission statement is one I may use. It is memorised because I choose to know my business mission/vision statement by heart. This helps me to use it to promote my business case verbally to a prospective client:

'Delivering services as a business trainer, coach, mentor, adviser and researcher to assist clients explore, exercise and examine vast business enterprise tools and methods to support their business and personal development. This represents your business aspirations and transforms your business from where you are today to where you need to be tomorrow and is also for your personal development'.

The above is just one of my business case and my elevator-pitches, which I share with you to assist you develop your own.

Now, what is your business case and elevator-pitch?

Your elevator-pitch is a statement or collection of statements that you need to develop which summarize the products or service you provide in your business enterprise.

It is a powerful marketing tool that you can utilize to make a quick case about your business to a potential investor, customer or other stakeholder.

Chapter 9   Your Business Starts Trading

It is usually followed by an exchange of business cards.

As a matter of business etiquette, never pocket a business card while the giver is still standing with you. Rather, examine it, make positive remarks on it and treat it with tender-loving-care TLC. Make a note with a pen to remind you if you need to take future actions and wait until the giver departs before you pocket it, remembering to follow it up with an email or phone call.

Still on business ethics, a confident, friendly, winning smile with reassuring eye-contact and firm hand shake, depending on the situation and person(s) involved, is a good way to effectively network, leading to new business conversations. You will be positively surprised when you start receiving phone calls from people who are interested in knowing and learning more about your business. This could be due to your practised, punchy elevator-pitch, winning business behaviour,

> *'Never pocket a business card while the giver is still standing with you. Rather, examine it, make positive remarks on it, treat it with tender-loving-care, then, wait until the giver leaves before you pocket it. Make a note to remind yourself should you need to take future actions and remember to follow up with an email or phone call.'*

charming smile, eye contact, confidence, professional exchange of business cards and the courage and confidence that comes from your good knowledge of your market sector.

Do not be surprised when you start receiving more traffic or hits on your website. These are the benefits experienced when you proactively structure and deliver your business case and elevator-pitch which are confident, trust worthy, useful and use both positive verbal and non-verbal language, all well represented.

I am a believer of the phrase, 'It's all in your presentation.'

Remember this when presenting to your market or advertising your business, e.g. presenting a business case and an elevator-pitch.

Most people learn better either through one of the following channels:

- Visual - by seeing
- Audio - by listening
- Kinaesthetic - by role play, combining audio and visual and feeling (at some level)

Always consider the following:

- Non verbal language – This is the interpretation which the audience you are presenting to will be receiving from your body language. It sends either positive or negative signals to the mind of your audience. For example, use

Chapter 9   Your Business Starts Trading

open handed gestures instead of closed; make eye contact and nod your head in agreement to what **you** are saying. Avoid gestures that could contradict what you are saying, rather, use gestures that further enhance your points, their potential, their potency and your positive persona

- Verbal language – Making an oral presentation is one part and connecting with your audience is another, essential part of using language. Using appropriate voice pitch to drive a point home, using an appropriate tone of voice, speaking clearly, concisely and using simple words that encourage and engage your listeners to pay attention all contribute to your business sales presentation.

'Most people learn better either by listening (audio), by seeing (visual) or by role play, which is a combination of audio, visual and touch (kinaesthetic).'

It is commonly suggested that your elevator-pitch should not exceed 30 seconds. However, it could be 50 seconds or even for as long as a minute; so far as the individual's attention and interest remain focused on your presentation. The only way you can have an idea of the level of your audience interest in your elevator-pitch is by developing the ability to multitask. What this means is doing more than one task at the same time: speaking to your audience whilst paying attention to your audience body language as it reacts involuntarily to what your are saying.

Some positive signs are:

- Smiles on their faces – could mean they are impressed
- Sounds of agreement – could mean, you know your subject
- Clapping and cheering – could be saying 'we are your top fans'
- Focused eyes and head nods – could mean we are in agreement

Some negative signs are:

- Wandering eyes from left to right – if they are paying attention to you, their eyes will wander less
- Scratching of their head – could be saying 'time-up'
- Rubbing of arms – could be their patience is running out
- Checking of mobile phone – could be checking for better things to do than listening
- Yawning and red eyes – could be boredom.

Be mindful, especially, that you don't waste their time. For them to start yawning at you shows how bored they are. The overall length of time your elevator-pitch takes is important. The selection of powerful phrases and words; the content of your message; the tone of your voice; the pitch of your voice and your body language are all very important.

Chapter 9   Your Business Starts Trading

Although your elevator-pitch may last for 30 to 60 seconds, as long as the individual(s) are interested, they will pay attention. Be prepared to take questions because they may use the information you have stated to clarify details of your business operation, forecast and benefits.

These methods outlined may enhance your marketing output, raise your business profile, gain funding from investors, promote your service and products unique selling points better and network effectively.

There may be occasions where you find the clients very interested and asking more questions. You must engage them and be willing and able to go into appropriate details to establish your business case. This is where you convey your passion, your operations, relevant finance and customer insight, in fact, knowledge of every aspect of your business enterprise.

I remember a certain media programme in which an entrepreneur was presented as seeking funding to start a business and was asked who the product was aimed at. The entrepreneur responded that the product was meant for everyone. The potential investors were alarmed because the product clearly suited only a specific gender and they refused to invest because they believed the entrepreneur had little or no idea of the target group and was, therefore, a huge business risk into which to invest their money.

Marketing your business is very important and needs financial budgeting and when you make a budget, be disciplined and stick to it. Make sure your marketing performance is recorded and reviewed regularly to analyse if the money, time and resources spent is value for money and meeting the expectations of your marketing plan.

'The duration of your elevator pitch is critical and the selection of powerful words, content of your message, the tone of your voice, the pitch of your voice and your body language is very important to maintain audience interest.'

Firstly, you need to understand who your potential clients are, so you can target that group of people. This is why the primary market research tools, e.g. questionnaires and secondary market research tools, e.g. online search of statistics from the chamber of commerce, etc, comes into play. The outcome of such research will help you understand what has been going on in and is current in your businesses' market environment and the consumption behaviour and pattern of your potential customers and it will also inform you on related or alternative services or products.

Market research will assist you to capture who your target

Chapter 9　Your Business Starts Trading

customers are, what they need, how much they may be willing to pay, who they are currently buying from, how best to reach them and how to add value to their needs.

Marketing is important to your business enterprise; it does not need to consume all your funds because you have to always find ways and means to save the pennies. Find creative ways and means to take care of these pennies, so the pounds will take care of themselves. Marketing is still very critical and needs to be managed at low cost but for high impact.

Advertising can be creatively managed. Many people have cars and have members of their family and friends who have cars. Sticking a professionally designed business sticker on a car windscreen can be a very useful advertising method at low cost but with high impact. Business people call this an unconventional method; creative advertising or guerrilla selling.

> *'Find creative ways and means to take care of the pennies, so the pounds will take care of themselves.'*

To enable the above method to have the impact you need, use the services of a professional designer to create a high quality sticker with high visibility. Then, get permission from your friends, colleagues and family to stick it on their car rear windscreens without obscuring their driving vision. The sticker requires carefully selected colours worded with basic information about your company name, products and services and necessary contact information like web address, email or telephone numbers.

You and your friends, colleagues and family members park your cars at different shopping centres, roads and areas of the country.

They drive their cars around towns and around cities and so do you. What the stickers on the cars are doing is giving you free advertisement. This would have cost you huge sums of money. Think of this and other creative methods to improve marketing and sales.

> **'Food For Thought: Market research will assist you to capture who your target customers are, what they need, how much they are willing to pay, who they are currently buying from, how best to reach your customers and also feed backs on your service to them.'**

Using business cards and word of mouth is still a useful, time tested and powerful tool for low cost advertisement and still a business-must-have.

Flyers and posters are still very effective marketing tools; though it greatly depends on what type of business you are operating and who your target customers are.

Chapter 9   Your Business Starts Trading

Supporting charity events within your local community, wider community or private and public organisations that you have (or can have) developed contacts with, is a good way of telling your target audience about your product or service's unique selling points.

You might demonstrate how your business product and service can add value to them in a better, cheaper or more sustainable way than the service or product they currently use.

Think of adopting the promotional method of giving sales discounts deals for a specific time for attendees at such charity events only. This method enables them to have a practical taste or experience of using your products or services during these events or for a set time or at a set venue after the event.

'Co-host events where you will be allowed, as a co-host to place your advertisement signs, e.g. placards, flyers, and posters in and around the venue with your business mission, vision statements services and contacts.'

Another creative method is to co-host events where you will be allowed, as a co-host to place your advertisement signs, i.e. placards, flyers, penguin stands and posters in and around the venue with your business mission and vision statements and with statements which show how your business adds value to customers needs. This has the potential to attract new customers and keep them as your business repeat customers, who then go on to become steady and loyal customers.

The importance of developing and having a fit-for-purpose website is a business need that will help you to have an anchor point where people can visit and find out more about your business. Here they will be able to relate to your products and services and correspond with you over twenty-four hours and seven days of the week. Customers may remember your business products and services and forget your business name or vice versa.

> *'Choose a business name that rings a bell, a name that portrays what your business does, a name that is meaningful to you and your business. Choose a name that is not already in use by another company with similar goods and services.'*

The reason I say this is that you should choose a business name that 'rings a bell'; a business name that portrays what your business does and a business name that is meaningful to you and your business image.

Naming a business with a name that could confuse your customers or a name that is already in use by another organisation may have legal implications. A name like XYZ&A International Partners may mean something to the business owner. However, at first glance, it may mean little or nothing to potential customers. Whereas a name like XYZ&A International Relocation Services makes more sense at first glance. In business, it is profitable to try to make impact at first glance and first opportunity.

Explore using the power of the internet to check if the businesses name you have chosen is already in use by another company with your kind of goods and services before registering that name. The process of registering a limited liability company (Ltd) is stringent than registering a sole trader business.

When you have decided on a business name, see if that business name is available as a domain name and invest in it. In the long run, it could save you time and money.

Apply the safe-web-name idea by choosing more than one domain name. An example might be if you choose to name and register your business name as: My Healthcare. The domain name may be available as: www.myhealthcare.biz. However, if it is not available as www.myhealthcare.com or www.myhealthcare.co.uk (dependent on the country domain where your business is located), it is suggested you think twice, because when potential customers use web search engines, they are more likely to be directed to the .com, .net .co.uk and .co web sites before the .biz web site. Your .biz web site may appear on the second or third page of a web search engine like Google™. My personal survey has shown that most customers doing web engine search, rarely check the second and third pages during a search.

Therefore, choose a name that allows you to at least purchase the .com or .co.uk and any other domain that you deem wise for your business plan and business locality.

Chapter 9

Your Business Starts Trading

Chapter 9

Your Business Starts Trading

Contenders versus Pretenders

IT REQUIRES A WINNING SPIRIT to get to a point where your business is open, willing and able to trade. Once you have reached this stage, it already shows your energy, endeavour and excellence to be successful in your business. When you get here do celebrate your journey for a minute and then, get back to work. Starting your own business must have been a remarkable journey and may have, surprisingly, exposed you to yourself in a way you never knew yourself before.

The business start date is not an end to itself, but a turning point. Now that you have started trading, selling and delivering goods and services you need to keep on improving your business activities.

At this point, it is important to recognise that you are no longer a surprise to your business competitors or to other new business start-ups that are about to start in a similar business sector. So, the protective cover you had before, from other businesses being unaware of you is now removed. Competitors may now study what you are doing well, what you doing poorly

Chapter 9 Your Business Starts Trading

and what you are not doing at all.

This is a time for you to minimise every possible cost without compromising customer satisfaction. It is a time when you do not only work harder but also work smarter to continuously develop yourself to improve your operations, build customer base, expand income and think how to make the next creative move. Learn to reduce expenses by a regular review of your suppliers and see what they and your competitor's suppliers are offering for the same service and price range.

All your business suppliers: electric company, banker, gas company, solicitor, business adviser, accountant, web designer, etc., should be reviewed regularly; at least twice yearly. Check if your bank is giving you the best interest rates and benefits. Check if your accountants are giving you the best price and service by speaking to other accounting firms. Check that your business adviser is giving you the best creative and strategic advice on the next moves required by your business to efficiently expand or maintain

'Time to work harder, quicker and smarter to continuously develop your self; improve operations; build customer base; expand income; reduce expenses and think how to make the next creative move.'

growth.

Find out which gas and electric companies will meet your business needs better and cheaper. Review your customer feed backs. Send your customers emails, updating them on new products, services and new deal offers. This keeps your customers thinking and speaking of you first rather than your competition.

Remember, if you do not review all the above operational costs, you may be losing money in your business bank account. When you don't communicate, negotiate and inform current suppliers that you have found other suppliers who are better and cheaper, you may keep losing money. Losing money constantly without a corresponding larger amount of income is not healthy for the growth of your business enterprise.

> *'If you do not review your operational expenses, you may be losing money and if you don't renegotiate with your suppliers when you have found another supplier that is better and cheaper, you will keep losing money.'*

When your business activities fail to practise the above, it may prevent your customers from receiving the best services at reduced cost.

Always appear professional and friendly with your suppliers.

Chapter 9   Your Business Starts Trading

But never be emotionally attached or get too friendly with them to the point where you lose the focus that you are in business to make profit and so are your suppliers. So do not feel so comfortable that you fail to check out other suppliers who can supply you the same goods and services cheaper and even better. Never allow your relationship with your business suppliers to deny you getting the best service at the possible lowest cost.

Developing good negotiation skills will really help you in managing your relationship with your suppliers. Remember, however, that the money you pay them is like a highway that drives money out of your business bank account.

The reason for this is that researching the market for better deals and learning how to negotiate with suppliers will keep extra money in your business bank account and so keep you smiling.

'Good negotiation skills will obtain for you good business contracts and remove from you bad business contracts.'

Regularly research your suppliers' charges and service quality and have the self-belief to negotiate a better deal, even with your bank manager. It will save you money and enhance service.

Some people have the attitude that some things are set in

stone, yes, some may be, but not all. You lose nothing in trying; rather, you gain something by making an effort. If your competitors are not good at doing this, you are on your way to reducing business expenses, which leads to more profit and business growth.

Therefore, learning how to negotiate with your suppliers and customers can get you into good contracts and out of bad ones.

There is some flexibility in being able to maximise prices of your services or products without being seen to over-charge your customers. Pricing your products and services can be a make or break for your business. Most customers will be unhappy if you charge them higher without exceptional value for money. On the other hand, customers will worry if you charge them a very low price for high quality products and service.

This is an aspect of how the human mind works. Even though the product or service is really cheap and better than others, they will doubt your intentions if the price seems too cheap. Customers may start worrying that there is a catch somewhere and may start distrusting your business intentions, or your product. At this stage of your business enterprise, continue with extensive marketing and have a marketing plan but stay within budget and review your marketing plans quarterly, depending upon your individual business needs. Continue to attract new customers, impress all customers and retain existing, loyal customers.

Chapter 9   Your Business Starts Trading

Remember that keeping current customers is more challenging than getting new customers. Current customers' positive feedback to their friends, associates and family about your services and products will lead to loyalty and repeat customers. Repeat customers occur when customers have bought and used your products and services, and are satisfied, and come back to do more business with you.

Repeat customers will most likely tell their friends and families about your products and services and this will attract them to use your products and services also, becoming your new customers.

'Remember that keeping current customers is more challenging than getting new customers and current customer's positive feedback about your services and products can lead to loyal and repeat customers.'

In my fifteen years of experience, I have learnt to get it right first time. It is appreciated by customers because it is seen as what the business is expected to do and customers will speak positively about the good products or service they have received or purchased from the business.

On the other hand, your customers, potential customers and market in general are more prone to talk, to a greater extent, about bad

- 113 -

services and products which your business has delivered. This is because it is not what is expected and will therefore make 'news headlines'.

If, at this point, you say it is a tough world out there, then you are not alone. Therefore, given the above human behaviour, do not **wait** for customers to say positive things to their friends and families about your product and services. They require additional motivation, otherwise they will naturally say very little.

What you can do is to use methods, like gift vouchers and discounts, to encourage your current customers. Enable them to receive specific benefits within a specified time period, if they invite their friends and families to use your services or purchase your goods.

If your customers are aware that they will get certain benefits from you when they invite their friends, associates and families to buy from you, it might be a strong, motivating factor for them to use word of mouth to others about your business. Better still, if and when you can afford it, give them flyers with links to your web site with discount codes so purchases can be made online at discounted price.

By doing this you are making good sales, attracting new customers, retaining old customers and expanding your marketing through trade discounts and gift vouchers for loyal customers.

Chapter 9   Your Business Starts Trading

Strategic calculations cost the discounts and vouchers for each old customer against the benefit of bringing a new customer. This new customer makes a specific number or value of purchases for the old customer to benefit from the discounts. The vouchers you have planned will still give you a great return on your investment.

Another secret is for you to insist that the trade discounts and gift vouchers are redeemed only at specific days and times. This could be the days and times when you have few or no customers. Through this way you are keeping your business traffic flowing wisely, you are busy and still making some profit instead of none.

The best hands in the business must be your target to hire. When you decide to hire a person they must be one who will maintain, expand and continue building your business enterprise ideas. Never hire based on anything but on the requirements of the role your business needs. If you hire wrongly, you will end up firing and if you fire wrongly you will end up at employment tribunal, not to mention the impact the aggrieved personnel may have on your business reputation.

Hiring a manager will be very helpful if you choose someone that shares your business passion, your business mission and your business values. It will also be based upon someone who will take your ideas further, and who will creatively work to transform your passion, mission and values into real operations that will yield sustained, successful results.

It is suggested that you avoid interviewing on your own and avoid interviewing potential candidates just once. A one-off interview may allow you very little chance to find out the qualities of the person you are looking to hire. Interviewing just by yourself may expose you unnecessarily, in that candidates who do not get the job may go on to complain that you were unfair to them and may bring up accusations ranging from race, sex, religious, and age discrimination.

For this reason you would be better safeguarded if you invite another one or two colleagues to support you, by being part of an interview panel and for whom you can do the same favour in return when they are hiring. This is another reason I encourage you to network and have professional colleagues whom you can use for interviews in a trade by barter system, as discussed previously. Hopefully, you may have colleagues with some experience in Human resources management to assist you with ethical and procedural issues.

Avoid simply calling the referees mentioned by candidates in their curriculum vitae, to only ask them to confirm if the individual in question can do the job. When you contact referees of candidates, remember that these referees could be just anyone and, if well structured questions are not used, will just tell you that the candidate is the best in the world!

In order to address this, you need to think outside the box and ask questions that will get the referee outside their comfort zone. Use a question style that will persuade them to give you

Chapter 9   Your Business Starts Trading

some more insights into the candidate's attitude, work rate and aptitude when under pressure. Plan ways to make referees feel 'safe' and inform them that whatever they tell you over the phone will remain confidential. You may be surprised to hear the real truth as to why the candidate lost or left their last job. This will help you to hire safely, keep your business culture and maintain winning business behaviour to **unleash your life's greatness.**

Chapter 10

A Final Note

Chapter 10

A Final Note

Never Work in Anyone's Shadow

This is a note for the great women and men who thought to have a business idea and who have the will and ability to fulfil that thought in enterprise. An enterprise is a project especially requiring boldness, originality and an adventurous spirit.

This note is also for those who tried but failed and have the courage to try again so as to go on to win; it is also for those who have won and for those who have the attitude to win again and again in business and personal enterprise.

It is for those with the energy and hunger to continuously develop personally, professionally and psychologically in business world.

I hope the content of this book has given you the energy to remember:

- If you can think it - you can make it happen
- If you seek knowledge - you will find it
- If you try - you can **unleash your life's greatness**

- If you stop procrastinating, fearing and doubting – you will win
- If you start thinking, acting, believing, living by faith and not by sight alone – you will fulfil your divine perfect purpose that you were created to fulfil

It is suggested to always apply profitable creativity and not to just act with the first thought that comes to your mind. Think of the impact it will have today, in the future and as judged by history.

A friend once said that we can choose to act in one of two ways. Either like a thermostat, which is set and automatically maintains the desired temperature. Alternatively, we can be like a thermometer, which measures the temperature. As a thermostat we define what we aim to achieve in business whereas a 'thermometer' measures others' successes or failures.

So, which of these two are you: a thermostat or thermometer? It is advisable to be successful and let others measure you, rather than measuring others' successes!

There is a saying that the current global economic climate is a time to try harder, work harder and dig deeper. It is a time for you to believe in your talents, your dreams and say to your self 'I am possible', no matter the challenge presented. In business, it is not a question of **if** there will be challenges, but rather, **when** will the challenges come.

Chapter 10 A Final Note

Learn to celebrate your business success and achievement. Manage your challenges and stay ahead of your competition and celebrate business success.

Remember, in every triumph, there is a trial. It is now your time, your choice and your chance to choose to make history or choose to make excuses. Which do you choose? I hope you will choose wisely to make history as you **unleash your life's greatness.**

Glossary of Terms

Glossary of Terms

Glossary data were obtained from www.businesslink.gov.uk, www.nightingale.com and www.businessdictionary.com

Budget - A planned outcome for your business to achieve and an outline of what you will spend your money on and how that spending will be financed. It is not a forecast, which involves a guess of future finance expectations.

Business - An economic system where goods and services are exchanged for other goods and services or for money, on the basis of their apparent worth.

Business Culture - Style of day to day activities within an organization, which determines how different levels of staff communicate with one another as well as how they deal with clients and customers.

Business Ethics - Written guidelines issued by an organization to its staff and management, to help them conduct their actions in accordance with its primary values and standards.

Client - Customer of a professional service provider, or the principal recipient of goods and services.

Business Operation - Activities involved in the day to day function of the business conducted for the purpose of generating profit and delivering services.

Competitor – Any company in the same industry or a similar industry which offers a similar product or service. Presence of one or more competitors can reduce the prices of goods and services as the companies attempt to gain larger market share.

Elevator pitch - Very short and snappy presentation of an idea covering all of its critical aspects delivered in less than a minute (the approximate duration of an elevator ride)

Enterprise - Entire business group or corporation comprising all local, international head, sub offices, divisions, subsidiaries and departments or fledgling new business start up.

Financial analysis - An assessment of the level of effectiveness raising, using and employing money in managing healthy business process that result in profits, losses and/or breaking even in business activities.

Gift Voucher – It is any substitute for money which could be used to pay for goods and services and often a form of credit.

Guerrilla selling - It is all about using unconventional process, plan, and policy to make sales consistently and increase sales income and profit. It's simple, inexpensive and adaptable.

Performance indicators - These are measurable ways to display the achievement of an outcome. They enable decision-makers to assess progress towards intended outputs, outcomes, goals, objectives, and are chosen to reproduce success factors.

Innovate - A process by which an idea or invention is translated into business goods or services to attract more people to pay for its reasonable price to satisfy specific need of users.

Investment - Money dedicated or property acquired for future business income.

Limited company - An incorporated limited liability firm whose ownership is through the share capital of one or more than one individual and management operations are restricted by its memorandum and articles of incorporation.

Limited liability partnership - Business structure that combines features of a limited company with that of a partnership for use as a tax shelter, but does not create a legal entity separate and distinct from its owners who are jointly and severally liable for all its debts and obligations.

Loss - An unrecoverable and usually unanticipated removal or decrease in possessions or resources used in managing business process.

Market research - Component of marketing investigation where a specific market is identified and its size and other characteristics are measured.

Marketing strategy - Written plan, usually a part of the overall corporate plan, which combines product development, promotion, distribution and pricing approach to identify marketing goals to explain how they will be achieved within stated time. It determines the choice of target market segment, positioning, marketing mix and allocation of resources.

NLP - Neuro-Linguistic Programming is a set of rules and techniques proposed for modifying behaviour in achieving self improvement, self management, and more effective interpersonal communications.

P.E.S.T.E.L - A technique for understanding the various external influences on a business.

S.W.O.T – An analysis to provide a clear origin for examining your business performance and prospects. It can be used as part of a regular review process or in preparation for raising finance or bringing in consultants for a review.

Pre start - Original stage in the life cycle of an enterprise where potential entrepreneur generate or notice business idea.

Profit - Best known measure of the success of an enterprise, it is the surplus remaining after total costs are deducted from total revenue, and the basis on which tax is calculated and dividend is paid.

SMART - A procedure for testing the various factors that control internal and external business goal setting

Sole trader - The sole proprietor or sole owner of a business or a self-employed person such as a grocer, plumber, or taxi driver. He or she directs the affairs of the enterprise, bears its risks and losses, and takes the profits and benefits.

Start-up - Early stage in the life cycle of an enterprise where the entrepreneur moves from the idea stage to securing financing, laying down the basis structure, and initiating operations or trading.

Supplier – Also called vendor, an external entity that supplies relatively common, off the shelf, or standard goods or services, as opposed to a contractor or subcontractor who adds specialized input to deliverables.

Goal - A goal is an observable and measurable end result having one or more objectives to be achieved within a more or less fixed time. In comparison, a 'purpose' is an intention (internal motivational state) or mission. The question, "Has the goal been achieved?" can always be answered with either a "Yes" or "No." A purpose, however, is not 'achieved' but instead is pursued every day.

Target -The finish line of a goal. The objective which is planned understood and intended.

Transaction - Agreement, contract, exchange, understanding, or transfer of cash or property that occurs between two or more parties and establishes a legal obligation.

Praise for Unleash your Life's Greatness

Praise for Unleash your Life's Greatness

"An excellent support for new and existing business people, who will be aided in developing their business skills and so improve themselves."
Vivienne Scantanbury, Business Consultant, Greater London Enterprise

"A powerful step-by-step contribution to the world of business enterprise for everyone, and this includes migrants, to transform their enterprise ideas into reality."
Austin Aneke, CEO UK Immigrant Magazine

"This easy to read business start-up guide will prove to be an invaluable and helpful source of ideas for entrepreneurs. The inspirational content will empower many to take their destiny into their own hands and help in fulfilling their dreams."
Gill Fennings Monkman MBE, CEO Counselling for a change

A unique and useful business support manual for new and existing business owners and managers which will help to improve their business acumen and expertise
Janice Beckles, SFEDI Business Consultant, Women Business Centre

About the Author

About The Author

UNLEASH YOUR LIFE'S GREATNESS BY **O.C. VINCE** IS AN EXCELLENT FOCUS FOR ANYONE WHO HOPES TO START THEIR OWN BUSINESS BUT IS HINDERED BY PROCRASTINATION, EXCUSES OR WHO LACKS INSPIRATION TO FULFIL THEIR POTENTIAL IN BUSINESS ENTERPRISE.

VINCE HAS OVER FIFTEEN YEARS OF EXPERIENCE AND ACHIEVEMENTS IN BUSINESS ENTERPRISE DEVELOPMENT, TRAINING AND MANAGEMENT WITHIN PUBLIC AND PRIVATE SECTORS.

EXAMPLES INCLUDE; BARCLAYS BANK PLC, CABLE AND WIRELESS (CW), UNIVERSITY OF EAST LONDON (UEL), GREATER LONDON ENTERPRISE (GLE) AND THE UK NATIONAL HEALTH SERVICE (NHS) AMONG OTHERS.

VINCE POSSESSES A DEGREE IN FINANCE AND BANKING, A POSTGRADUATE QUALIFICATION IN BUSINESS MANAGEMENT, A MASTERS IN CORPORATE FINANCE AND LEGAL GOVERNANCE AND IS CURRENTLY PURSUING A PHD. CURRENTLY HE IS THE DIRECTOR OF ENTERPRISE CONSULTANCY, A COMPANY FOCUSED ON DELIVERING WINNING BUSINESS **SOLUTIONS**, PEOPLE AND PERFORMANCE DEVELOPMENT **TRAINING**, BUSINESS **PLANNING** AND **FACILITATION** FOR CORPORATE ORGANISATIONS. EXAMPLES OF THESE ORGANISATIONS INCLUDE GLE, ONE LONDON, FAMILY MOSAIC, WOMEN BUSINESS CENTRE, BARCLAYS BANK AND LONDON BOROUGH OF SOUTHWARK ETC.

THIS BOOK WILL HELP YOU MASTER THE PROGRESSION OF YOUR SKILLS, TALENTS AND IDEAS INTO SUCCESSFUL AND PROFITABLE BUSINESS ACTIVITY TO UNLEASH YOUR LIFE'S GREATNESS.